A Manager's Guide to Saying and Doing the Right Thing

I quit.

101

Ways to Lose a Great Employee

Barbara Otis

To my husband, Peter, for always believing in me and telling me,

"There's no one better to invest in than yourself."

Every workplace seems to have a go-to person—someone outside the typical chain of command or office hierarchy who possesses a magical combination of perspective, wisdom and experience upon which to draw and help you with an issue. You can bring nearly any problem, personal or work-related, to this person and know you will receive expert advice and assistance. Often this person is not at the top of the organizational chart, but has his or her finger on the pulse of the organization and knows exactly how it's run. What you get from this person—without drama or fanfare, and in an objective, logical manner—is spot-on advice about how to deal with anything and everything.

Barbara Otis is one of these people—and one of the best go-to people I have ever met. Her career trajectory has seen her ascend the ranks of both private and public-sector organizations, and she has developed an uncommon amount of common sense. She has heard nearly every workplace tale of woe that requires a friendly ear, and along the way she discovered that most of these unfortunate situations involved questionable management behavior.

As she skillfully kept her coworkers off their proverbial ledges, Barbara collected a long list of dubious management practices that she had helped coworkers cope with—or had experienced herself. She noted how often these practices were creating a wedge in these employees' loyalty and productivity and, in short, driving them away. It turns out that what should be common sense when one human manages another simply isn't, and her list grew and grew. She has now compiled the most common and egregious of the items on her list in book form, and the book you are about to read is the result of that effort.

As you read through this book, you will realize that you are not alone. Nearly every employee has been on the receiving end of at least one of these mistakes, and these managerial blunders are more wide-spread than you think because managers are fallible human beings.

Clearly there are better ways to manage employees. For each entry, Barbara describes more successful approaches. In reading through them, you may be inspired to find new ways to facilitate constructive change in your organization.

If you are a manager and find some of your actions reflected in these pages, take a deep breath and realize that no one is perfect and it is difficult to behave optimally in every situation. Use it as a guide for self-evaluation and a roadmap to creating better relationships with your employees. If this list of "thou shalt nots" too closely resembles your personal management style, then it's definitely time to rethink your practices. Should you ever find this book on your desk with pages tagged or highlighted, pay attention. It's a sign that you're driving people away from your organization.

Sloane Valentino
Captain, Tiburon Fire District

Acknowledgments

To my family and friends: Thank you for your encouragement, support and humor through this process. I couldn't have done it without all of you.

To Julie Prime: Thank you for your excellence in editing and making my work shine brighter than I ever thought it could.

To Kristie Hansen-Kemp: Thank you for your creativity and for bringing the book to life with your expertise in graphic design.

To Sloane Valentino: Thank you for writing the foreword to this book. You uniquely summarized and shared the essence of this book in a way that only you could do.

To Kimberly Richardson: Thank you for sharing your brilliant skills in photography. You really captured my personality.

To Dr. Vicino, all of my instructors and my Institute for Leadership Studies cohort at Dominican University in San Rafael, California: Thank you for your support and belief in me.

Finally, to everyone out there trying to make a difference in their work environments: Don't give up! This book is for you.

Why write a book on how to lose a great employee? During years of witnessing problematic interactions between managers and members of their staffs and dealing with the fallout, I observed how frequently inattention to good management practices resulted in devastating effects on those involved in the exchanges—as well as on those around them. Through both inadvertent and deliberate actions, managers were driving employees away from their jobs, destroying morale, and often changing the entire trajectory of a team or organization in a negative way. Shockingly, they often had no idea they were doing it.

Even managers who had good intentions were making big mistakes, sometimes because they had let their guards down and acted without thinking through the consequences and other times because they thought that their misguided management styles were somehow going to achieve their desired results.

Because so many people were suffering from these managerial misbehaviors, and because so many organizations were being damaged, I wanted to call attention to these issues and the huge negative impact they have on productivity. I wanted to make people aware that even the seemingly smallest oversights—such as never smiling or saying good morning to your employees—can end up having significant ramifications.

The place to realize your style is driving people away is here. The time to change it is now.

People are first and foremost human, yet in work environments we tend to focus on the technical aspects of people's skills and abilities. In reality, a corporate culture includes much more, such as how our feelings and behaviors impact everyone around us. To understand the ripple effect of people's behavior is to begin to understand what is known as emotional intelligence. While I talk about it in regard to managers in this book, the concept applies equally to all employees.

Comprehending the power of emotional intelligence can be a true asset. When you actively pay attention to the emotional intelligence factor at work in your organization by identifying and assessing your own emotions and those of others around you and by purposefully choosing how you act in encounters with your colleagues and employees, you will see positive results, real progress and greater success.

Consider this book another step in a lifelong journey of learning. I encourage you to become familiar with the emotional intelligence model and to develop your leadership skills through other modes of learning. Let this book be a catalyst for you to think about how your actions and reactions are affecting others. The lesson here is twofold: Great managers strive continuously to improve their management techniques, and they apply what they have learned day in and day out—for each day brings new opportunities to fortify or damage their connections with their employees. Building solid working relationships takes work, training, patience, perseverance and attention to even the smallest details.

If you find that you are exhibiting any of the behaviors described in this book, consider it your wakeup call—and an opportunity to begin improving the quality of your relationships with your employees. Don't risk losing your best employees due to bad habits that you have the power to change.

People often ask me whether the examples listed in this book really happened. I assure you they did, and there are hundreds more I could add—many of which would also make you wonder what those managers were thinking when they chose to act the way they did.

I will close with a quote that sums up why I wrote this book:

"I've learned that people will forget what you said, people will forget what you did, but people will never forget how you made them feel."
–Dr. Maya Angelou

Barbara Otis

During interviews, tell candidates what you think they want to hear.

Once they're hired, don't follow through on anything you said you would do.

Say anything and everything to get potential employees to take the jobs you are trying to hire them for. You need bodies to fill the seats, and once they're hired, they're yours. Your plans are grand, your intentions are good, and you know you should actually do the things you talked about. So what if your follow-through is less than stellar? They couldn't possibly remember everything that was said in their interviews.

Instead:

Be honest during interviews as to what you can and cannot offer potential employees, and don't make promises you can't keep. Why start off a working relationship with either a lack of commitment to what you said—or downright dishonesty?

Never say good morning to your employees.

If you do, you're admitting that you're at their level–that you're "one of them." It's best to keep them guessing as to whether you respect them.

Passing your employees in the hallway without acknowledging them and avoiding common courtesies such as saying hello will help keep them in their rightful place–beneath you.

Instead:

Take the time to greet your employees. It's free, it's easy to do, and it has a positive impact on how they view themselves and their value in your organization. Being "seen" is a basic human need.

Never smile.

Showing emotion is regarded as weak.

Smiling in the presence of your employees? Never a good idea. It's best to keep a scowl on your face. You don't want to show your employees that you have a human side. They may begin to view you as being weak.

Instead:

Smile, laugh and be appropriately friendly with your employees. Sharing the lighter side of your personality costs nothing and will help create a feeling of camaraderie within the group and convey the message that you are a team.

4

Never make eye contact with your employees when you speak to them.

That's way too personal.

Always look down at the ground, off to the side or over their heads when you speak to your employees—never straight in the eye. This will serve as a constant reminder that they aren't important enough to look at or pay attention to, and it also makes it easier for you to lie to them.

Instead:

Look your employees in the eyes when you engage in conversation. It's a sign of respect, your communications will be much more powerful, and you'll maintain better business relationships with them.

Speak to people in a demeaning, condescending tone.

Public humiliation increases your power.

Intimidating others and making them feel dumb and inept is most effective when done in front of a group of colleagues. Everyone will want to stay on their best behavior so they won't have to endure your wrath, and your actions will have an additional benefit: Employees will feel incompetent enough that they will forever be on a quest to please you. Their constant striving will make you feel powerful, but of course they will never be able to satisfy you because you will always find ways to keep them from believing that they have met your standards.

Instead:

Speak to your employees in a respectful tone and manner. Acknowledge good ideas, make individuals feel that they are an important part of the team, and support them in their efforts to do their best for you. The goal is to draw people toward you, not push them away.

Always dominate the conversation.

It'll make you seem like the most important person in the room, and you really don't want to hear what others have to say anyway.

Your ideas are far better than those of your employees, so why let them have the airtime? Interrupt their thoughts midsentence, and talk louder if they don't stop talking. This accomplishes two things: It reduces the amount of time wasted in discussions and meetings, and it discourages them from speaking up again.

Instead:

Welcoming employees' contributions in meetings and conversations makes them feel like their opinions and ideas are valued, so listen carefully to what they have to say. You may learn something new or solve a problem in a way you wouldn't have thought of.

Use intimidation tactics such as yelling, frowning and crossing your arms over your chest.

Appearing aggressive and confrontational will help keep employees in their place.

Use threatening movements and gestures and changes in the tone of your voice to continually keep your employees on edge. Frown at them in meetings and project an image of being closed to what they would like to say so that they will stop talking, feel uncomfortable and become insecure.

Instead:

Pay attention to your body language and how you're speaking when you address your employees and colleagues. Crossing your arms over your chest suggests that you are unapproachable. As a leader, you want to appear open to ideas and input, not closed-minded.

Be a bully.

Being nice never got anything accomplished.

Torment your employees on a daily basis by threatening them with the loss of their jobs, embarrassing them in public and calling them names. Some will end up with little to no self-confidence; others will learn from your behavior and become "accessory bullies" who can help you inflict your brand of misery.

Instead:

Unless you want to find yourself involved in a lawsuit, change your ways quickly and stop bullying. It only takes one employee to stand up and say no to abusive behavior, and typically there is at least one hero in every organization.

Don't give your employees the resources to do a good job.

It will only fuel an endless desire for more, more, more.

Additional support or resources are a drain on the budget. If your employees can't accomplish their work with what is currently available, too bad. With any luck, when they hear you say no enough, they will stop asking.

Instead:

Provide the tools and resources your employees need to do their jobs. Your support will grease the wheels of productivity and help make your employees feel heard and motivated.

Impose unreasonable project deadlines.

Speed is more important than quality.

Badger your employees to get their jobs done fast and meet your deadlines at whatever the cost—even if your deadlines are bogus. It's not important that they do their jobs right the first time; it's essential that they do them quickly. If they miss the mark the first time, they can work nights and weekends to fix it.

Instead:

Don't make every job a rush, or you will exhaust even your highest achievers. Prioritize tasks realistically, and create a healthier work environment by putting structures and procedures in place to assist employees in meeting deadlines while maintaining a high quality of work. While deadlines are certainly important, keep them achievable.

Don't go out of your way to help your employees become successful at their jobs.

If they don't know what they're doing, that's their problem.

People create their own destiny in this world. It's not your responsibility to help your employees be successful at their jobs. You pay them to show up, shut up and do the work. It's really simple when you think about it.

Instead:

Look for ways to help your employees become successful at their jobs. It is your responsibility to provide your employees with appropriate support so that they can produce the high quality work you desire.

Withhold important information.

They don't need to know everything.

Don't tell your employees everything they need to know to do their jobs well. That takes all the fun out of watching them struggle. Consistently withholding valuable information related to work assignments will help secure your position, as they will always need to come back to you to request additional information—even to get the simplest of tasks completed. Hoarding information brings you power.

Instead:

Share with your employees all the information necessary to complete a project. This isn't about you—it's about the success of your team and the organization. Holding back information may make you feel needed, but it sabotages success.

Make yourself as unavailable as possible.

Leave them guessing as to where you are and when you can see them.

Lock yourself in your office, avoid contact with your employees, and never be available to answer any of their questions. It's best to keep them guessing as to what you are doing–out of sight and out of mind.

Instead:

Be available to answer questions and share important information with your team. Keep them informed about critical decisions regarding programs and projects that impact their work. Helping them do their jobs successfully is your job.

Ignore your employees' emails, phone calls and voice mails.

Responding would interfere with making progress on your own agenda.

When your employees send you emails or leave voice mail messages, ignore them. You don't have time to respond to every question or request. Eventually they'll get the message that no response will always be your response, and they'll leave you alone. With any luck, they may even forget about their requests, just as you have.

Instead:

Reply promptly to communications from your employees. Constantly ignoring their requests for information and delaying decisions are ill-mannered habits that show them you don't value their priorities enough to respond. Even if you don't think their messages are important, they do—and they're waiting for responses from you.

Constantly reschedule meetings.

Your employees should work around your priorities.

Your time is more important than anyone else's on the team, so feel free to reschedule meetings whenever your priorities shift, cancel them at the last minute or forget to cancel them altogether so everyone ends up waiting for you in a conference room and wondering what happened. Eventually they'll figure out you're not coming. So what if they waste a half hour of their time? It'll probably give them a good chance to relax.

Instead:

Make every effort to attend meetings with your employees. Certainly there are times when rescheduling can't be helped, but if you are doing this regularly, you need to stop this rude behavior—before your employees begin to think that you are "crying wolf" every time you do schedule a meeting. Leaving your team waiting for you is disrespectful and a waste of time and resources.

16

Check email, send text messages and take phone calls during meetings with your employees.

They don't need your full attention.

You're a key player. Your time is valuable and in short supply. That's why it's okay to multitask if an employee starts blathering on about something unimportant to you in a meeting. At least you'll get something accomplished, and hopefully they'll eventually get the message that they should be more interesting and move the discussion along.

Instead:

Your time with your employees is important. They wouldn't be requesting a meeting if they didn't feel they had something important to share or discuss. Not staying "in the moment" and providing them with your full attention leads to frustration and a feeling of being disrespected. It also could result in misunderstandings that are costly to you and the organization.

Interrupt employees to correct them when they are giving presentations.

The audience needs to know that they don't know what they're talking about.

Against your better judgment, you let one of your employees make the presentation to a senior management group or important client. While they are presenting, interrupt them to clarify the material or point out that what they are presenting is wrong. Do it in a humiliating way so the presenter's confidence is destroyed. Then, to make sure everyone knows who really possesses all the knowledge and talent on the team, jump in and take over the meeting.

Instead:

Meet with employees in advance of important presentations to review their agendas and key points. Discuss any changes before each meeting to ensure everyone is on the same page. You will show your employees that you care about their success, and you won't come across as an overbearing boss who doesn't trust his or her employees.

Micromanage.

Employees are incapable of managing their own time and work.

You're responsible for everything, so everything should be under your control. You know you've been successful at micromanaging when your employees feel as if they should call you to get permission to use the bathroom.

Instead:

Give your employees the autonomy to make decisions on their own regarding their work. Empowering employees helps build their confidence, fosters creative thinking and promotes productivity.

Remind your employees daily who the boss is.

Knowing the pecking order will help keep them in line.

How dare they start to act all high and mighty? Who do they think they are? The ones in charge? If you don't remind employees that you're the boss, they may start to feel that they are smarter than you or have skills or ideas to offer that you do not.

Instead:

Explore opportunities where your employees can lead projects and gain exposure to other types of work that will increase their knowledge, skills and abilities. Let someone else be "the boss" for a while. Cultivate a sense of ownership over work projects and being successful. Effective managers help to develop in others the leadership skills that benefit their teams.

Put an end to laughter.

When they're laughing, they're not working.

If you hear laughter, take steps to stop it. What could your employees possibly be laughing at? You maybe? Whatever they're laughing at, it's unacceptable. Work isn't about having fun, it's about working. It's best to reprimand this type of behavior by making them work overtime or piling on more work with shorter deadlines. They'll soon get the message that if you have time to laugh, then you have enough time on your hands to do more.

Instead:

Join in the laughter when appropriate. Be a part of your employees' conversations. Humor is a good thing in the workplace. A team that laughs together often forms a closer working relationship.

21

Regularly tell your employees that they don't know what they're talking about.

Make them afraid to make a move without your consent.

By frequently degrading employees, they will begin to believe you. Their self-confidence will erode, and they will become paralyzed professionally—afraid to make a decision without your input or approval. Their abilities to think and act creatively will be squelched, reducing the risk that they will ever outshine you.

Instead:

Respect your employees' points of view. Validate their contributions, and look for common areas upon which you can agree.

Point out to your employees the things that they don't know and probably never will.

They need to know they will never be as smart as you.

Regularly remind your employees that they are not subject-matter experts in their jobs. You know how to do your job—plus the jobs of everyone else on your team. Remind them that you have the history, experience and education that they will never possess, and that you are the holder of all knowledge. In fact, they should just call you "guru."

Instead:

Let your employees know that you value their education, skills, knowledge, experience and expertise. You can't possibly do all of their jobs better than they can.

Tell your employees that you don't like their work, but never tell them why.

It's best to keep them guessing.

Not giving your employees details about their performance deficiencies keeps you in a powerful position because if they don't know exactly what they're doing wrong, they'll never have opportunities to improve. Persist with this behavior, and you can continue making them feel inadequate and devalued for years.

Instead:

Regularly provide feedback to your employees and have any difficult conversations regarding work performance sooner versus later. Collaborate with them on a plan for improvement, with defined goals, dates for completion and consequences if they are not able to improve. Everyone deserves authentic feedback and opportunities to do better.

Ignore any ideas or suggestions your employees submit for your consideration—and never ask them for any.

Who cares what they think?

Asking employees for their opinions is risky business. After all, what could they possibly have to add? Your opinions should carry the most weight, and using their input could potentially make you look bad and make others think you're not doing your job well. Avoid activities that solicit feedback, and disregard your employees' suggestions unless their ideas can be used to boost your own power and image.

Instead:

Know the skills and talents of your team and seek out their opinions. You never know who will come up with the next great idea or the solution to a problem. When your team does well, you'll look good too.

Have your employees do their work—plus take on your responsibilities too.

They have nothing better to do.

Whenever the opportunity arises, transfer the majority of your work to your employees. Senior management doesn't care who's doing the work as long as it gets done. Freeing up your schedule will give you sufficient time to plan your next vacation, surf the Internet and catch up on personal emails. You'll look like you've been working all day, and the work will get done. That's what's most important.

Instead:

Don't load up your employees with work responsibilities that belong to you. Be the leader you should be and take responsibility for the work that is truly yours.

Ask employees to run your personal errands.

They're there to help you, aren't they?

You need to pick up your dry cleaning, get tickets for a show and take your dog to the groomer. How can you do all this and put in a full day's work? The answer is simple: Get your employees to help out. They're headed out to lunch anyway. Why shouldn't they run quick errands for you? The projects you're working on are way too important to be interrupted by such menial tasks.

Instead:

Take care of personal errands yourself and stop devaluing your employees' time. They're called personal errands for a reason. They are your responsibility—not your staff's. If you really do need the help, hire yourself a personal assistant.

Insist your employees accommodate your constant procrastination.

So what if it habitually results in inconvenient overtime?

You do everything at the last minute, so what's the big deal about having employees put in overtime to accommodate your incessant lateness? Be sure to drop the overtime requirement bombshell on employees late on a Friday afternoon. Then leave explicit instructions as to what you want accomplished as you walk out the door to enjoy your weekend. You'll find out who your allies really are by watching to see who will acquiesce to your demands.

Instead:

Don't surprise your employees with last-minute overtime requests. Plan ahead, inform your employees and be sensitive to the fact that they have their own lives. If overtime is required, make sure you're doing your fair share.

Constantly reorganize your department or team.

Frustration is a good motivator that will toughen up your employees.

You hear that companies are reorganizing all the time, so it must be good—right? Reorganizations prove you're a mover and a shaker. Don't worry if you have assigned people to jobs for which they are not qualified or lack the skills to perform. You'll just change their roles again in a few months anyway. And while reorganizing may cause confusion as to what your vision is and where you are going as a team, it will help keep your employees on their toes.

Instead:

As a leader, you have to adapt to changes in business. While this may mean reorganizing at times, don't overdo it. Reorganize with care, have a clear implementation plan to share with your employees, and communicate in a timely, effective manner about the changes. If you don't, even employees who enjoy working for you might become frustrated enough to leave.

Don't show any interest in what your employees are doing at work.

You don't have time to monitor them.

Ignore your employees and their job responsibilities. Try to get out of managing them as much as possible. Who cares what they are working on, as long as they are not at your door bothering you? You have better things to do.

Instead:

It's your job to know what your employees are doing. That's why you are called a supervisor or manager. You need to know more than just the basics so you can track progress and provide guidance when needed.

Never say thank you.

It's overused and overrated.

You don't need to say thank you to your employees. Why would you? You hired them; they work; you provide a paycheck. End of story. If they are waiting for a thank you from you, they're going to be waiting a long, long time. It's not your job to feed their egos, and if they don't like it, that's their problem.

Instead:

Say thank you when appropriate. People need to feel acknowledged, and a simple thank you costs nothing but goes a long way toward making people feel they're valued.

Never tell your employees that they have done a great job.

You're the only one who really does good work.

Why would you ever tell an employee they're doing well? What are you thinking? If you tell someone that you think their work is good, they'll expect praise—and a raise.

Instead:

Acknowledge a job well done. Employees need to hear positive comments from their managers and will appreciate recognition when it is genuine.

Don't acknowledge hard work or dedication.

You work harder than everyone else, and you don't hear people applauding for you every day.

Even when employees on your team have shown terrific dedication through hard work and commitment, don't call attention to it. It's much better in the long run for your team to labor hard and long in total obscurity. It builds character. Besides, you work harder than any of them. Whatever success your team has is because you are carrying them on your back.

Instead:

Acknowledge contributions appropriately and express gratitude for your employees' hard work and commitment to the team's success. All your employees need to hear that their efforts are noticed and appreciated, and a little recognition goes a long way.

Don't give employees individual recognition.

No one is that special.

Never single out an employee for commendation; you don't want to imply that one person can stand out from the rest of the team. It's best to keep recognitions to the group, even though some individuals may not have done anything to deserve the acknowledgement.

Instead:

Take the time to recognize individuals independently for their successes. Not all employees produce equal amounts of work, and employees who work hard to achieve superior results should be shown appreciation for their efforts. Acknowledging accomplishments might even inspire others.

Never take employees to lunch.

They can buy their own.

If you take one employee out to lunch, you'll be setting off an avalanche of trouble. Soon others will be expecting it and will feel slighted if you don't choose them. And think of all the money you'll be wasting. If you must show your appreciation, do it in a way that doesn't cost you anything or create unnecessary expectations.

Instead:

Take your employees out to lunch periodically. It's a great way to get to know your staff, build rapport and engage with them on a different level. If you don't have the financial means to pay for their lunch, split the ticket.

Don't deal with the problem employee.

Maybe the issue will resolve itself.

If you have an employee with whom you need to have a difficult conversation, avoid dealing with the issue as long as you can. If you can't avoid it, get someone else to talk to them. Conversations like these are too uncomfortable and time-consuming. You don't have the energy or desire to talk about unpleasant matters, and even worse, listen to people defend themselves. Just sweep the matter under the rug and pretend everything is okay.

Instead:

If you know something is wrong, have the difficult conversation. Typically even the individual who is involved knows that they deserve to be called out on their behavior. Ignoring it only prolongs the problem and makes you look weak as a leader to your employees.

Speak negatively about your employees when you know they can overhear.

This clever tactic will help you avoid confronting people who aren't making the grade.

When you're unsatisfied with an employee's work, discuss it with his or her peers while making sure you are within the employee's earshot. Talk about how inefficient and unproductive this person is, and be sure to get into specifics about what you don't like. By doing this you will reveal your real feelings about the employee's performance without needing to have a face-to-face confrontation. This method also inflicts a dose of humiliation and helps create low self-esteem.

Instead:

Be cautious when you are speaking about your employees. If you feel the need to vent to another colleague about your frustrations, it's best to do this in a closed office where your employees can't hear you. Remember: Your employees are real people with real feelings.

Never let your employees have a flexible workweek.

If they want flexibility, they can go find other jobs.

Be tough about this: Employees should be at their jobs during the normal work hours created by the organization. If people want flexibility, then they shouldn't have taken the jobs. Besides, if you show them leniency and let them do it once, they'll never stop begging for more. Where would it end? Anarchy would ensue, and it would be difficult to ever rein them back in.

Instead:

In today's employment market, embracing flexibility in your work environment helps attract the best and the brightest talent to your organization. Flexibility doesn't mean less work; flexibility can trigger greater productivity because your employees are happier, more fulfilled, and can develop an increased sense of loyalty to the workplace. Who doesn't enjoy being given more freedom and control over his or her own schedule?

Express your disapproval of breaks.

Encourage goofing off?
Are you kidding me?

Seriously, why would anyone ever need a break at work? Employees should be sitting at their desks, producing work at warp speed and leaving their desks only to take bathroom breaks or to eat their lunches. Why would you ever act like you approve of them being unproductive? When people stand around, they chat. Talking leads to gossip and rumors, and those types of conversations lead to dissatisfaction and problems.

Instead:

Encourage breaks so employees can replenish their energy. Create a break room so people have a place to step away from their desks to take breaks or eat lunch. You'll find that you'll have a more creative team of employees, and they'll have more stamina to power through the day productively.

Don't allow food or drinks at your employees' desks.

They can eat and drink on their own time.

Allowing food and drinks at your employees' desks is an invitation to waste time and a hazard to the machinery, furniture and flooring when they inevitably spill what they're consuming. Every sip of tea or coffee represents time stolen away from work, and the additional garbage it creates makes more mess for the custodial staff to clean up. Employees should do all of their eating and drinking during their breaks and lunch hours.

Instead:

Allow drinks and snacks at your employees' desks. You'll be surprised how something so simple can increase productivity.

Discourage fitness-related breaks.

Employees can get healthy on their own time.

B y all means, don't encourage employees to take walks or utilize your organization's gym or fitness room. Your employees are there to work—not exercise. And if they think you approve, then it might become a habit that continues wasting time on a regular basis.

Instead:

Support your employees' desire to step away from their desks for a quick walk or workout. Physical activity helps keep your employees healthier and stimulates creative thinking.

Ask your employees to work late while you go home.

They don't have anything better to do.

All of your employees need to learn that the boss never stays late. You climbed the ladder to management so you wouldn't have to work late any more. That's for people beneath your level and frankly one of the perks of being where you are now. Get your underlings to do all the hard work for you.

Instead:

Stay late to help your employees with rush projects or assignments with looming deadlines. They will see you as a real partner and someone who will stay in the trenches to collaborate with them when the going gets tough.

Insist that your employees carry their cell phones and check email after hours.

You're busy working after hours, so why shouldn't they be available to help you out?

Technology makes connecting with your employees exceedingly easy these days, so whenever you have ideas you want to bounce off them, or need answers about projects, just call or text them—even if it's after hours or late at night. It won't take them that long to answer, and you will reach a higher level of productivity. It will also help you identify which employees will go the distance for you. Be sure to show them that you're angry if they don't respond—or don't respond quickly enough—to your messages.

Instead:

Unless it is a true emergency or part of a mutually agreed-upon arrangement, don't text or call your employees after working hours or expect after-hours communications from them. Your employees deserve a break and will feel more refreshed and ready to take on their assignments if you allow them some time to rest.

43

Always say no when your employees ask for time off, no matter what the circumstances are.

They don't work hard enough to deserve time off.

Discourage employees from taking time off. If you're in the office, they should be in the office. What if you needed something from them and they weren't there?

Instead:

Encourage your employees to take time off now and then to show your staff that you care about their well-being. They will return to work rested and re-energized and have more positive attitudes about their jobs.

Make employees work during their vacations.

Then charge them their full vacation time anyway.

So what if your employees are on vacation? You need things done right, and done right now. While they are gone things just don't run as efficiently, so call them. Text them. Email them. Tell them that they'll need to participate in conference calls, attend meetings, produce work or do research while they are taking vacation time. Make them do enough to keep your work life running smoothly. Too bad if it interrupts their plans and makes them feel as if they've never truly had a break.

Instead:

In today's 24/7 work environment, employees need to have opportunities to switch out of work mode. If there are true emergencies that require their participation, notify them as far in advance as possible and work together to determine the best solutions.

Don't let your employees take vacations during specific time periods.

So what if they have important personal plans during that time?

Work comes first in your life, and it should take top priority in your employees' lives too. They must accommodate your needs—and one of those needs is to have them avoid taking vacation time during specific periods. If that means they can't take summer vacations with their families while their children are out of school or attend family weddings, then so be it. Be sure to break the news about this new requirement at the last minute. It will eliminate much of the whining and complaining you might otherwise be forced to endure.

Instead:

Try to be as understanding as possible about your employees' needs, but if there are work responsibilities that require employees to be at the office during a specific time, share this information as far in advance as you can. Your employees will be more willing to accommodate your parameters, and it may give them sufficient time to make alternate personal plans.

When your employees are out sick or in the hospital, encourage them to keep working.

Why waste all of that downtime?

When an employee goes out for surgery or an extended medical leave, work around "the system" to keep them productive. Even if they are in the hospital, they can still participate in conference calls and respond to questions. There are laws relating to this, so you will need to be in stealth mode when setting up your arrangements. Make your employees feel as guilty as possible—and tell them that they are leaving you in the lurch.

Instead:

Never expect your employees to work from home or the hospital when they are out on a medical leave. They are on leave for a reason. Show some respect and kindness. Not only is it the right way to handle the situation—it's the law.

Never let your employees travel on nonessential business trips.

They are not important enough.

Never allow your employees to travel to trade shows, off-site business meetings or to the corporate office. They are not professional enough to engage in business travel, it costs your department money that could be better spent in other ways, and you'll have no idea what they will do or say when they are out of your sight—and control.

Instead:

Allow your employees to travel to appropriate business meetings, trade shows and other important meetings. Your investment will make them feel that you trust them, value their contributions, and support their desires to sharpen their skills and broaden their perspectives.

If your employees must travel for business, make them pay for it out-of-pocket—then wait a month or longer to reimburse them.

You pay them a decent salary, so what's the big deal?

Place the burden of travel expenses on your employees as much as possible. It's more convenient for you to deal with reimbursement on the back end rather than providing corporate travel cards or purchasing tickets with company funds. Besides, chances are they will lose some of their receipts, which just means more money for your organization.

Instead:

Be mindful and considerate of the fact that some of your employees do not have the funds up front to spend on business travel. You may find that more of your employees may be willing to travel if the funds aren't coming out of their pockets first.

Insist that your employees dress professionally, but don't pay them well enough to do it easily.

Seriously, did you see what they were wearing?

Dress codes are important for your organization, but should you really have to foot the bill by giving them sufficient pay to do it? You see them going out to lunch and spending their money foolishly. It's their problem—typically a lack of control—if they don't have enough income left to dress the way you think they should.

Instead:

Make sure that your employees' salaries reflect the requirements you have for them to look professional. Explain to your employees that projecting a professional image is important not only to the organization, but as a means to enhancing their own image as well. Dressing well—and appropriately—will help them to be seen as professionals by their colleagues, internal leaders and external customers.

Pretend like you know what you're doing.

It doesn't really matter that you don't, does it?

If you don't really feel that you can manage a particular project, wing it. Pretend to know what you are doing. Provide incorrect information and poor guidance to your employees. When your employees or others confront you, turn on the supportive manager act and lie like you have never lied before.

Instead:

If there is a project you feel inadequately prepared to handle, search for the right resources on your team to step in and help— or hire external subject matter experts. No one can know or be an expert on everything. Employees respect leaders who can stand up and say, "I don't know the answer, but I'll work with you to identify our best options."

Don't give your employees credit for their work.

They're only successful because of you.

Take credit for all of the good work that your employees produce. You're the leader, and they couldn't have achieved any success without your expert guidance and support. Be sure that none of your employees are around when senior management recognizes you for a job well done, otherwise they will know that you didn't acknowledge anyone on your team.

Instead:

Acknowledge your employees when they perform well. Your team members will feel valued for their contributions and respect you for your honesty and generosity.

Pass your employees' ideas off as your own.

A chief benefit of having employees is to make you look good.

When an employee on your team shares a good idea with you, use it to your advantage. Shouldn't brilliant ideas really be coming from you anyhow? Your employees are really just there to implement your vision, so never pass up the opportunity to take one of their winning ideas and submit it as your own.

Instead:

Give credit where credit is due. Recognize the contributions of others and what they bring to your team, and create a safe and supportive work environment where people feel comfortable sharing.

Don't help your employees advance in their careers.

Why invest time or money in their professional development when it could result in them leaving?

Remind employees about the skills and professional education they lack so they'll think that they'll never be able to move beyond their current positions. This will help ensure a low turnover rate in your group, making you look like a successful leader with excellent retention of staff. Besides, why should you be responsible for orchestrating career development plans for your employees? They should be happy with what they do now.

Instead:

Ask your employees if they would like to grow professionally in their own jobs or potentially move up the ladder, then find ways to make it happen. By doing so, you will inspire them to work hard, and you will attract other achievers to work for you. Advancement is a part of life.

Discourage employees from participating in special projects outside of your authority.

You wouldn't want them to outshine you.

If you let employees participate in projects outside of your control, they'll share their ideas, skills and talents. Your colleagues may begin to view them as important contributors. These employees may start to think they really do have value, which might make them want to jump ship and join another team. You may lose them.

Instead:

Encourage your employees to share their knowledge and subject matter expertise across the organization. Having a team where people feel confident about their skills and abilities to contribute stimulates creativity and productivity.

Only print business cards for supervisors and managers.

No one else is important enough.

Only provide business cards to your organization's management team. It will help you create a culture of "us vs. them" and help keep employees in their rightful places. By not having business cards, the lower level employees will know they are less valuable.

Instead:

Provide business cards to everyone and level the playing field. You don't have to have a fancy title to be important in an organization.

Never introduce your employees to anyone else in your organization.

Yours should be the face that represents your group because no one is as important as you are.

Introducing your employees to anyone else in a leadership position within your organization is asking for trouble. What if they make solid connections with the other managers? What if they end up on friendlier terms with your colleagues than you are? What if their talents overshadow yours? To be safe, you are the only individual who should socialize at this level.

Instead:

Introduce your employees to other leaders within your organization—and appropriate external customers or clients as well. This will make your employees feel valued and respected and give them a more complete picture of where they fit in the organization and what they can do to help it succeed.

Don't speak about your employees in a positive light to other associates.

You wouldn't want anyone to think that individuals on your team are more capable than you are.

If you speak fondly of your employees, you might give the impression that they are the true force behind your success in the organization. It's best to tell everyone that without your leadership they couldn't get anything done on their own.

Instead:

Speak positively about your employees with other leaders in the organization. Others will see that you are connected with your team, know their skills and utilize their potential to achieve successful results.

Never refer to your employees by their names.

You don't want to appear as if you know them that well.

Always refer to an employee on your team as "my employee" when introducing this person to others inside and outside of your organization. There is no need to use first or last names. You wouldn't want others to think you are friendly with the people who work for you. You want to establish and reinforce the pecking order.

Instead:

Introduce your employees to others by sharing their first and last names. Everyone deserves to be known for who they are as individuals. And besides, this is a common courtesy that will reflect badly on you if you overlook it.

59

If you see one of your employees speaking to your colleagues, ask what the conversation was about.

They might be talking about you.

What could employees who speak to your peers be talking about? Troubles with your team? Problems with your leadership? Transferring to another department or resigning? The best move when you see your employees speaking to colleagues of your pay grade or higher is to immediately take them aside and ask them what they were talking about—then shame them for wasting the time of these important people and advise them never to do it again.

Instead:

If you see one of your employees speaking to one of your peers, don't say anything. What they are discussing is none of your business. Employees have a right to speak to anyone they want.

When employees get promotions into other departments, make them feel as guilty and undeserving as possible.

Who do they think they are, leaving you?

Why be supportive of employees who get transferred or promoted into other departments? Downplay their achievements by telling them that you have wanted to get rid of their positions, and you were only doing them a favor by having them in your group in the first place. Their promotions are meaningless. It doesn't mean that they did good work; it only means that they will become some other managers' problems now.

Instead:

Acknowledge your employees' promotions. If someone on your team receives a promotion or advancement and you respond positively, you'll have a better chance of retaining their goodwill— and they will never forget your supportiveness.

Always inform other supervisors and managers about what their employees are doing.

They need help handling their employees.

Your peers will appreciate knowing information about their employees, such as whether they are taking longer-than-necessary lunch breaks, what types of cars they are driving and people they are seen talking to. You know—the important stuff that managers need to know about their employees.

Instead:

Don't gossip to your peers about their employees' everyday activities. Your peers were hired to manage their groups; you should be managing yours. If another manager's employee is causing problems for you or your team, or you become aware of a serious issue such as harassment or criminal behavior, by all means speak up.

Don't provide any training.

They should have the skills for the job already.

Why should you pay for training for your employees? You hired them because they have the skills to do the job. You're not running a university, and you're certainly not going to pay for employees to better themselves on company time. Either they know what they're doing or they don't. If they don't, they can leave.

Instead:

Offer training opportunities for your employees. Whether it's a refresher course or training for a new skill, you will be showing your employees that you value their work and have an investment in their future with the organization.

Don't encourage higher education or advancement.

It's not your job to support your employees' dreams or aspirations.

If employees go to school in the evening, make it as difficult as possible for them to get to their classes on time. Ask them to stay late when you know they have to leave. Purposely give them projects that will interfere with their schedules. Increase the pressure, and make them feel that they will need to quit their educational pursuits to please you. Tell them you need them to be focused on their current responsibilities. You pay them, and you should be their highest priority.

Instead:

Encourage higher education and learning with your employees. Talk with them regarding their work schedules, and don't sabotage their dreams even if you don't believe in them.

Don't support employees when they come to you with work-related problems.

If they don't know how to do their jobs, that's their problem.

Don't assist employees in finding solutions to their work-related problems. They need to figure it out on their own and stop bugging you. If you knew they were going to be this much trouble, you would never have hired them in the first place.

Instead:

All employees benefit from having bosses who are understanding of their learning curves, and with seasoned employees, some issues are better solved collaboratively. Employees typically don't like going to their bosses with problems, so remember that they have probably done everything else they could before coming to you. Support your employees when they come to you with work problems, thank them for bringing the issues to your attention, and help them work toward solutions.

65

Never have your employees' backs.

You're not taking the blame for anything.

If trouble arises, throw your employees under the bus. You never touched it, never heard about it and certainly did not approve of whatever they did. They are expendable; you are not. You didn't rise up through the organization by protecting people from the consequences of their actions, so why start now?

Instead:

To move any organization forward, it's necessary to try new things and take some risks, and some of these attempts will fail. Support your employees in taking initiative and encourage them to think creatively. Go to bat for them if their efforts result in any unforeseen problems, and you will gain their respect and loyalty. Having to deal with occasional setbacks is better than having a team that won't try anything new for fear you will hang them out to dry.

Never let go of a mistake.

Forgiveness is not an option.

When employees make mistakes, bring them up every chance you get. Everyone should know what they did and how you feel about it. Publicly sharing your dissatisfaction with a less-than-satisfactory performance works wonders for deterring future mistakes.

Instead:

Stop reminding employees over and over about their errors. No one is perfect. When people make mistakes, help them use it as a learning experience and move on.

Deny your involvement when your instructions cause problems.

Why should you take the heat when you could successfully deflect it onto someone else?

If your instructions lead to something going wrong, run the other way. Act like you never told your employees to do things that way. Make the problems seem like they were your employees' ideas. Do whatever it takes, but never take the blame for what they did—even though it was exactly what you told them to do. It might ruin your image.

Instead:

Take responsibility when your employees are carrying out your directives. Be professional, ask for their problem-solving ideas and engage their assistance as you move forward to fix whatever went wrong.

Identify your employees' vulnerabilities and use them to create insecurity and increase your power.

Know what pushes their buttons.

Find out what makes your employees feel uncomfortable, then use this knowledge to get what you want from them. Learning their vulnerabilities places you in a powerful position. For example, if you know someone has a weak spot in their command of a particular topic, call it out in front of coworkers on a regular basis to keep that person's self-esteem and confidence low.

Instead:

Handle your employees' vulnerabilities with care. Help them bring out the best they have to offer, and look for ways to help them overcome their limitations and insecurities.

Have an open-door policy, but discourage your employees from using it.

Listening to their silly little problems is such a drag.

When employees come in to talk with you, pretend to listen and be interested while they're prattling on about things you don't care about or want to solve. What you're really doing is thinking about how to get rid of them so you can go back to doing what you were doing before they came in and wondering why you ever mentioned an open-door policy in the first place.

Instead:

Establish an open-door policy where employees either feel welcome anytime—or have a scheduled appointment to discuss their issues. Even if their problems don't seem that critical to you, taking the time to listen and discuss the issues will make them feel like their thoughts are important and they are being heard.

If it's to your benefit, break an employee's confidentiality.

Nothing is really confidential in a work environment anyway, is it?

When one of your employees comes to you and asks to speak with you confidentially, always say yes, knowing that nothing is really ever confidential and that you will use the information to your benefit whenever the right opportunities come along.

Instead:

When an employee asks to speak with you confidentially, it is appropriate to preface the conversation by letting him or her know that you would be happy to keep the conversation confidential—unless the information shared involves something illegal, puts someone's safety at risk, or is in some other way inappropriate to keep private. Once you break confidentiality, your employees will be hesitant to share anything with you in the future—and will most likely never trust you again.

Never ask how your employees are doing.

Who cares?

Really, who cares how your employees are doing? You don't. People shouldn't come to work to be cared about. That's not what work is about. It's about getting the job done and not needing to be coddled while doing it. If your employees want to be doted on, they should look to their families and friends.

Instead:

Open yourself up. Ask your employees how they are doing and show them that you are genuinely interested in their lives. People will not stay with organizations if they do not feel valued or cared about. This doesn't mean that you need to go overboard, but showing real interest in their well-being and feelings is not only appropriate, but helps create healthy working relationships.

Tell your employees you don't care about their personal problems.

You're not their therapist.

Work is work, and what isn't work shouldn't be brought into the workplace. You have plenty to do every day without listening to your employees drivel on about their personal problems. If they have family issues, so what? Who doesn't? Those are problems that need to be left at the door and solved after hours. You should also find ways to deter your employees from sharing their endless stories with their coworkers.

Instead:

Life happens. People have problems. Employees and their family members become ill. While you don't want to take on a role as therapist, you should show your concern in a professional way and let them know you care. If referring them to your company's employee assistance program is appropriate, that may be a way to help without becoming personally involved.

Never ask your employees what they enjoy doing at work.

Tell them what they like doing.

You don't want to know what your employees enjoy doing at work. It doesn't matter because you don't care. Tell them how much they're going to like working on a project, even though you know they won't because it doesn't fit their skill set. So what if they're miserable? Work is not about being happy or satisfied.

Instead:

Figure out what your employees like to do, what skills they possess and what their strengths are. Assigning work in accordance with your employees' abilities and passions will inspire achievement, boost success rates, improve employee satisfaction, and cultivate a culture that respects and values what each individual brings to the table.

Avoid employee satisfaction surveys.

You don't really want to know what they think anyway.

You're getting pressured to do an employee satisfaction survey, but avoid it as long as possible. If you're forced to, go ahead, but don't do anything with the feedback since you're really not interested in anything your employees have to say. You're only conducting the survey to satisfy a business requirement and appear as though you care.

Instead:

While you won't be able to do something about every suggestion or complaint, surveys can provide a roadmap to cultivating more satisfied, productive and loyal employees. Review the feedback carefully and use it as a guide to help shape and improve your organization.

75

If your employees complain about something, purposely do more of what they don't like.

They'll think twice about speaking up again.

If employees think your office is too hot, turn up the heat. If the building is too cold, turn on the air conditioner. If they think they have too much work, load it on even more. Proactively punishing them will surely stop their whiny behavior and get them back to the important task of doing their work and making you look good. Never respond to their complaints; they will feel justified, and the demands will never stop.

Instead:

Listen to your employees when they have a complaint. Often it takes quite a lot for an employee to even bring an issue up to their immediate supervisor. Listen and discuss options for resolving the matter. Your staff will respect you for listening, even if you can't solve the problem.

Don't create employee incentive programs.

You wouldn't want to give the impression that you value your employees' work.

You already pay your employees, so why do anything else? It's a waste of time and money. Your employees were hired to work hard and perform well, and a job well done should be satisfaction enough. Besides, if you open the door to creating incentive programs, they'll never be satisfied without them. It's a slippery slope to be avoided, and the money it will take to create them will never be recouped.

Instead:

Incentive programs don't have to be costly to be effective, so work to establish something appropriate for your organization. Encouraging and rewarding hard work cultivates a sense of satisfaction and loyalty within individuals and teams and helps them to feel appreciated and valued for their contributions.

Never discuss corporate culture with your employees.

What the heck is it anyway?

Corporate culture is a popular buzzword in management, and you don't really want to know what it means. If you did, you might have to do something about it. And whatever you do, don't ever bring the subject up to your employees. They'll latch on to that cockamamie idea, and you'll be stuck with yet another responsibility.

Instead:

Corporate culture is the collective behavior and attitudes that characterize both your specific group and the entire organization. It's the undercurrent that can help make or break your success. Learning how to create a corporate culture that supports, inspires and motivates is crucial to success. Cultivating, ignoring or tolerating a negative corporate culture increases the risk of losing your highest achievers.

Don't respect cultural diversity among your employees.

If they want to dance to the beat of their own drums, they can find someplace else to do it.

When your team includes employees with different beliefs, backgrounds and cultures, be sure to let them know that you expect them to leave their individual ways of life at the door and follow your leadership style whether it works for them or not. You're not a member of the United Nations, so why should you care about trying to understand anyone else's point of view?

Instead:

Work to develop a clear understanding of your own culture and background—including morals, values and beliefs—and how these impact your leadership style. Then, open your mind to learning about the individual cultures within your team. Ask appropriate questions in a professional manner, educate yourself and, most importantly, listen. A team becomes stronger when its members respect and care about each other.

Ignore the value that different generations bring to your workplace.

Only listen to people from your generation.

Disregard the opinions of long-term employees who have worked for your organization or industry for many years. Obviously they have nothing new to add and are resistant to change, settled in their ways and biding their time until retirement. Younger employees, or those new to the organization, can't possibly possess the knowledge or experience necessary to add anything of significance, so discount them too.

Instead:

Embrace the different generations on your team. Celebrate their wisdom. Long-term employees have a wealth of knowledge and history about the organization and industry that you may never have. New employees may contribute fresh perspectives and relevant experience, and younger employees can bring innovative ideas and creativity to your group, sometimes with fewer inhibitions and biases.

Hide all information and marketing materials related to ergonomics.

They don't need any special equipment.

Don't mention or share any information about ergonomic furniture. Ergonomic furniture is expensive, and once one employee gets a special chair or device, others will surely want similar items. If an employee brings up the topic of physical discomfort in their work environment, change the subject quickly.

Instead:

Listen to your employees if they are having discomfort with their physical work environment. Beyond simply being sensitive to their needs, the law requires you to provide your employees with the ergonomic furniture they need so they can be comfortable and productive in their work environment.

Ignore the requests employees make for new software or upgraded computer equipment.

If you don't understand the need for the technology, and it doesn't help you directly, then they don't need it.

There is an endless number of ways to spend money on computer software and hardware, so why should you get snookered into buying the latest and greatest? There will just be another upgrade coming out tomorrow—or another piece of equipment that will be better, cheaper and faster.

Instead:

Using technology wisely can help employees produce better results and be considerably more productive. Review your employees' requests for computer-related purchases seriously. If you don't understand the technology yourself, seek out an expert from within the organization, or outside, to help you evaluate their needs and determine the best solutions.

Make employees clean their own office spaces.

Why pay someone to clean the office when everyone could just pitch in?

Hiring a janitorial service to clean your employees' offices is expensive. It's their space, so they should be responsible for emptying the trash, cleaning the windows, dusting the furniture and vacuuming the floors. Think of how much money you'd save on an ongoing basis, and think of how much cleaner they'd keep it in the first place, if they were responsible for cleaning it up. Besides, having them do menial tasks will help keep them humble.

Instead:

Hire a custodial service to do the regular maintenance of your employees' offices. Your employees will feel like their time is valued, and having a clean and tidy office space will help cultivate a sense of pride in their workplace.

Make your employees purchase their own office supplies.

If they want something special, they can buy it themselves.

If employees want something other than standard office supplies, let them purchase it themselves. Why buy specialty items that you consider to be frivolous purchases? After all, you're not running an office supply company. If you give in even once, there will be no end to their requests.

Instead:

Listen to the needs of your employees and provide them with the appropriate tools and resources to produce their work. If having a special office supply would boost someone's productivity, it might be worth it to be open-minded and compromise a little.

Insist that your employees adhere to arbitrary rules.

It's your team, so they should follow your wishes.

Make your employees follow meaningless orders from you that make no sense at all to them, such as only permitting them to use blue ink pens, because that's what you like. So what if enforcing oddball requirements such as this makes your employees rub their heads in confusion at the level of micromanagement you impart upon them? You're the boss, and they're supposed to do what you want them to do.

Instead:

Let employees use the tools they want unless there is a requirement for something specific, and keep in mind that people do not thrive under micromanagement. Pick and choose your battles carefully. Before you nitpick, ask yourself: Is this really that important?

Intimidate your employees into spending time with you outside of work.

So what if they don't like you or have other priorities for their free time?

Insist that your employees spend time with you after hours even if you know they don't want to. Getting them to believe that you are their friend will help you collect valuable personal information that you can use against them—and to manipulate them—in the future.

Instead:

Don't force your employees to spend time with you outside of work. If it works out, that's great. If they don't want to join in, don't punish them for not wanting to participate. They have their reasons, and their reasons are none of your business. Maybe they prefer their personal time to be just that—personal. When spending time with your employees outside the workplace, be careful to avoid crossing professional boundaries.

Don't allow your employees' families or friends to stop by the workplace.

You're not running a social club.

Why should employees' family members or personal friends stop by the office? You don't care about your employees' social engagements, and you don't want them interfering while your team members are trying to get their work done. Discourage this behavior by being rude and inconsiderate to your employees if they attempt to introduce you to their guests. If your family and friends stop by, however, that's okay. You're the boss.

Instead:

Let employees' family members and friends stop by the office occasionally. Most employees enjoy sharing the personal side of themselves with work colleagues, and having important people in your employees' lives be welcome in the workplace is appreciated.

Don't allow personal photos to be displayed.

They can see their family and friends when they get home.

Family, friends, pets, blah, blah, blah. You don't know most of these people or pets. Why should you be subjected to looking at pictures of a bunch of faces you don't know—or events you weren't a part of? Photos clutter up the office and make it look too homey and unprofessional.

Instead:

Allow appropriate, tasteful photographs of family, friends and pets at your employees' desks. Incorporating a little bit of home and having a few personal items in the workplace can help employees feel more content throughout the workday.

Never celebrate birthdays.

You're not their parent.

Why acknowledge employee birthdays? Who cares about their birthdays as long as they remember yours? After all, you're the important one. Without you, there would be no team. And besides, if you do it for one employee, they'll all want something special on their birthdays. What will be next? Anniversaries? New babies? Truly, the list of celebrations, which waste your organization's time and hurt productivity, never ends.

Instead:

Acknowledge birthdays and other special personal and professional events such as certifications, graduations from college, marriages and new babies—even if it is in a modest way. It builds camaraderie within your team and helps foster a harmonious relationship between you and your staff.

Don't allow flowers on your employees' desks.

The smell bothers you.

That's right, no flowers allowed. You don't like the smell, so all of those Valentine's Day, birthday and wedding anniversary deliveries to the office need to stop. Remember, it's all about you. Why are they sending them to work in the first place? Can't they send them to their homes and be done with it?

Instead:

If it's consistent with office policy, allow flowers and plants. They can brighten an employee's day and are a reminder that people care for them.

Single out one person as a favorite.

Make sure everyone knows who it is.

One of your employees is just more fun to work with than the others. Single this person out for frequent one-on-one meetings in your office. Supply this employee with ample rewards, such as easier schedules and extended lunches. Your employees will quickly see who is favored, and they will want that same special treatment and relationship with you. Instead of being focused on their work, they will concentrate on how to become the next favored employee.

Instead:

Interact with employees without showing favoritism. All employees want to feel that they have opportunities to excel and be rewarded for their contributions, so recognize employees who go above and beyond via suitable reward and recognition programs.

Groom one of your employees to be a confidential informer.

Everyone profits from a little inside information.

Select an employee to be your spy—someone you think is vulnerable to manipulation. Start exchanging office gossip, and let this person believe that the information he or she provides is invaluable to you. Over time, ask your budding snitch to listen to specific employees' conversations and report back anything he or she learns about the people you want to track closely. Before long, you will have your own personal mole within the team.

Instead:

Do not condition employees to reveal information about their colleagues or listen to gossipers who may spin damaging rumors within the organization.

Promote employees just because you like them personally.

So what if they don't really deserve the promotions you gave them?

You like these people. So what if they're unproductive, unqualified, disagreeable or snarky? Your style might make other employees in your department think your motto for promoting is "suck up, move up," but that's what works best for you.

Instead:

Cautiously and purposefully select deserving individuals for promotion on your team. Remember that others are watching, and the future success of your department depends upon having people in roles that suit their skills, experience and abilities.

Never promote camaraderie within your team.

They might gang up on you.

Socializing among employees is dangerous because they may develop friendships or alliances and form unflattering opinions of you as a leader. This could be particularly problematic if you know you're doing something unscrupulous or undesirable and notice that a majority of your team seems to feel the same way about you. Avoid dissension among the ranks by discouraging any type of bonding between employees.

Instead:

Encourage social interaction among employees. Oftentimes one of the best things about working in an organization is the people.

Eavesdrop on your employees' conversations.

They shouldn't be talking if they don't want you to hear.

It's essential to know what your employees are talking about, so hide behind doors or cubicle walls—or walk up slowly and stand behind them in a crowd—whenever the opportunity arises to snoop in on their conversations. Sneakiness pays off; you never know what valuable information you will learn.

Instead:

Don't eavesdrop on your employees' conversations. Not only it is unprofessional, but your behavior will be annoying and appear paranoid. Eventually, they may even start making up stories for you to overhear just to teach you a lesson.

Go through your employees' desk drawers when they are away from the office.

They've got to be hiding something.

When your employees leave for the day, for vacation or are away on a business trip, take a stroll past their workspaces, read the items on top of their desks and peek inside their desk drawers. After all, if they leave something at the office, isn't it fair game for anyone to look at?

Instead:

If you have time to snoop around your employees' desks, perhaps you don't have enough to do. Respect your employees' privacy—including their workspaces.

Make employees listen to your annoying jokes (even the ones about them).

They shouldn't be so sensitive.

Everyone knows you're a funny person and love to tell a good joke. You need to test your new material out, so corral your employees at least once a week to share the latest inappropriate joke you've heard. Better yet, make a wisecrack about one of your employees while that person is listening. They'll all get the message that no one is safe from being singled out.

Instead:

While everyone likes a good laugh at work, be careful about telling jokes—and never tell them about your employees. Something that you find humorous and innocent could be extremely hurtful or damaging to the person you target.

Regularly complain about your organization and job to your employees.

Misery loves company.

Yes, you are miserable, and venting your frustrations to your employees helps ease the burden. In fact, you feel best when you can hold employees captive in your office for hours, sharing your disgust for your manager and the disdain you feel for the organization and all the buffoons you must work with on a daily basis. If your team could only understand how difficult your job is, they would understand why you are so negative and hard to work with.

Instead:

Work to resolve problems and move forward instead of staying stuck in the status quo and bellyaching to everyone around you. If you must express your frustrations, speak in a professional manner with a peer or your boss about the issues you find concerning. If your problems seem insurmountable, maybe it's time to rethink your approach—or your role in the organization.

Foster an unethical work environment.

If you don't get caught, then it's okay.

Encourage your employees to take unethical risks that could potentially be damaging to them and the organization. You get a rush out of living on the edge, as long as it is someone else who is actually the one in danger.

Instead:

Never encourage unethical behavior in your employees or conduct yourself in an unscrupulous manner. Going against organizational ethical codes of conduct is a quick way to lose your job. If you wouldn't want your boss to find out—or read about your antics on the front page of the newspaper—don't do it.

Ask your employees to lie for you.

No one will get hurt, right?

Ask your employees—especially those whom you have befriended—to lie or cover up for you when you make mistakes or poor decisions. It will be difficult for them to say no to you because you will hold your position and friendship over their heads. This plan works especially well if it involves unethical behavior and you involve your employees in the unprofessional behavior as well.

Instead:

Never ask your employees, or anyone else, to lie for you.

Give your employees increased responsibility, but don't pay them more for it.

You've been doing extra work without extra pay, so why should they get higher salaries?

Why reward your employees with increases in incomes when you give them additional responsibilities? Taking on more work is the nature of how businesses operate these days. If they question you about raises, explain to them that doing more comes naturally with their jobs. Hopefully they'll be satisfied with that explanation so you can keep taking advantage of them.

Instead:

Show your gratitude when your employees take on more responsibility. This recognition doesn't always need to be in an increased income, but some type of concrete appreciation will go a long way toward building an excellent working relationship. Think outside the box. Maybe it's a small, one-time bonus—or a special lunch out with you.

Inflict performance punishment on your highest achievers.

They like to work hard, so why not pile it on?

Always overload your highest achievers with projects. They thrive on doing their best. You know you can count on them. You know they will get the job done right, and you know their exemplary work will make your team look great. So why shouldn't you take advantage of their strong drive and stellar work ethic? You know your other employees are slackers, and giving the work to them will be fruitless. So what if the lazier employees come to work, do as little as possible and still get paid? At least your work will be done well.

Instead:

Hold all of your employees responsible for their own work. Don't shift the load and overburden your best employees just because they are your highest achievers and you think your less productive employees won't perform adequately. Even devoted employees can burn out from feeling overworked, underappreciated and tired of unfair treatment.

Barbara Otis has a BA in Business Management from Dominican University of California, an MA in Human Resources and Organizational Development from the University of San Francisco, and nearly 20 years of experience in the field of training and organizational development. She develops training strategies and approaches, designs and develops training curricula, performs training needs assessments, maps work-flow processes and is experienced in workplace interventions and group facilitation. She also offers coaching and support to managers and employees for leadership development, change management and individual career development.

Barbara has received a Leadership Certificate from Dominican University of California, has completed The Making of Leaders program and is certified in the Myers-Briggs Personality Type Indicator® (MBTI®) personality inventory instrument. She is currently a member of the American Society for Training and Development (ASTD) and the Organization Development Network (OD Network).

Barbara lives in Marin County, California, with her husband, Peter. She invites readers to contact her at botis@comcast.net and visit her website at www.iquit.net to share their stories and get the latest news on *101 Ways to Lose a Great Employee*.

Made in the USA
San Bernardino, CA
07 January 2015